Best Practices for Fundraising Success
Diversifying Giving Channels

Authors

Katya Andresen

Melissa Bank Stepno

Amy Braiterman

Danielle Brigida

Mark Davis

Casey Golden

Tom Krackeler

Susan Ulrich McLaughlin

Katherine Swank

Curt Weeden

2012

D0169701

blackbaud®

Table of Contents

Introduction

Multichannel Fundraising: Best Practices Pay Long-Term Dividends

Chuck Longfield, Chief Scientist, Blackbaud

Fundraisers have been asking for donations since the dawn of time, employing new strategies, revenue streams, and communications channels along the way.

In ancient Greece, the wealthy donated to the building of temples and theaters, motivated by peer pressure and high ideals. From time immemorial, religions have raised funds for places of worship and to help the poor, calling on donors' relationships with a higher power. American colonists solicited funds for schools and fire engines, citing the greater good.

In 1865, the Salvation Army used personal appeal letters to raise money, food, and clothing. The Civil War fueled women-led fundraising fairs and bazaars, and the First World War saw the rise of nonprofits here and abroad, committed to supporting soldiers and affected citizens. They used word of mouth, events, posters, newspapers, and film. Radio appeals during World War II raised millions.

In 1917, Girl Scouts began selling cookies to their friends and neighbors, and early in the century, direct mail emerged as a powerhouse — an emotional appeal, an address, a stamp and fundraising was revolutionized. In the 1940s, television gave rise to the telethon, and in the 1990s Greenpeace popularized street-corner fundraising. Telemarketing was hot on its heels, and then the World Wide Web changed it all again by enabling one-to-many communications. Today, social media empowers new networks and channels in ways that we're still trying to understand.

It's an innovative history, but in every case, the early adopter was quickly copied by thousands of others, reducing initial gains. Discouraging? Quite the opposite. Our willingness to share what works is one of the strengths of our industry, because it allows us to identify and implement best practices — techniques that consistently deliver better results than other methods.

The trouble is, too many of us don't follow best practices.

The medical industry, for example, has a number of best practices that are routinely ignored. Boston surgeon and Harvard professor Atul Gawande found and reported that while hand-washing is a proven best practice in reducing patient infection, doctors wash their hands only one-third as often as they are supposed to, resulting in thousands of unnecessary infections and deaths.[1]

Our own industry has a classic example. A number of years ago, Penelope Burk, president of Cygnus Applied Research, Inc., wrote about the importance of thank-you calls in retaining donors. Through research, she found that when nonprofits call new donors to say "thank you" those donors feel significantly more valued and reward the organization with increased loyalty and money. In fact, there is a direct relationship between thank-you calls and the following year's giving — donors who received thank-you calls give 40 percent more the following year.[2]

I have repeated this research many times over the past two years, and have found similar results. And yet, in my work with clients, I see very few organizations that consistently make these thank-you calls.

While there are any number of reasons why people and organizations don't follow proven best practices, there are always more reasons for people to do so. It improves results in hospitals, in nonprofits, in the airlines, and in other industries.

Today's fundraising landscape is complex and changes quickly. To navigate in this new world, we need to follow best practices, to share our experiences, and to benchmark our results.

In this book, industry experts share proven best practices for various channels and revenue streams; the information has been broken down into easy-to-adopt guidelines. I hope that it will help you as you set strategies and plan your campaigns and events.

In summary, I would like to thank all of those who have generously shared their experiences and best practices with us. It strengthens the entire industry and positions us for a future that will be assuredly even more complex.

1. ATUL GAWANDE, Better: a Surgeon's Notes on Performance, Metropolitan Books, 2007.
2. Penelope Burk, Cygnus Applied Research, Inc. History of Direct Mail, Direct-Mail.org, Duneroller Publishing, http://www.direct-mail.org/history3.htm

Recommended Reading
1. The Pre- and Early History of American Corporate Philanthropy, Benjamin J. Soskis, PhD, the Center for Ethical Business Cultures, http://www.cebcglobal.org/uploaded_files/pdf/Soskis_-_History_of_Corporate_Giving_wp_final.pdf.
2. The SOFII History Project, The SOFII Foundation 2010, http://www.sofii.org/taxonomy/term/315 Rallying a Nation: American Red Cross Advertising During World War I, http://www.aef.com/on_campus/classroom/case_histories/3002.
3. Women in the American Civil War, Lisa Tendrich Frank, ABC-CLIO, 2008.

Chapter One

Peer-to-Peer Fundraising: Turn Constituents into Advocates and Advocates into Donors

by Amy Braiterman, Principal Strategy Consultant, Blackbaud

Today, peer-to-peer fundraising is practiced primarily by voluntary health organizations, but the strategy is becoming increasingly popular with community, arts, cultural, environmental, faith-based, international aid, higher education, and other organizations. Why? It's simple — by incorporating peer-to-peer fundraising into your existing marketing programs, you can increase revenues without significantly increasing costs.

Here's an example. Let's say your zoo is raising money for a new elephant exhibit via a brick-buying campaign. While you've offered engraved bricks at $100, $250, and $500, the reality is, not everyone can afford a $100 brick. So ask yourself: How many of my volunteers, members, and visitors could raise $10 from ten family members to buy a $100 brick? How many could raise $25 from 20 family members and friends to buy a $500 brick? Most likely, many of them could. What you have to do is give them the opportunity and the support to fundraise for your cause.

In this chapter, I outline five best practices for a successful peer-to-peer fundraising program, offer tips on how they can be integrated into your campaigns, and provide examples of organizations that are successfully using peer-to-peer strategies.

The benefits of peer-to-peer fundraising

There are many benefits of peer-to-peer fundraising, including relative low-cost, productive personal appeals, and extended reach into the community.

Low-Cost Appeals: Today, peer-to-peer fundraising is often done online, which generates interest in an organization at little to no cost. Management is done via a website with online tools, significantly reducing the cost of operation. A great example: The University of New Haven Athletics program was raising money in a variety of ways from membership dues to bake sales to annual campaigns. Adding an online peer-to-peer fundraising component to these existing campaigns proved inexpensive and effective. By sending emails and connecting with their social networks, student athletes were able to meet their fundraising goals.

Personal Appeals: Another benefit of peer-to-peer fundraising that is often overlooked is that it's personal so giving is less likely to be influenced by the economy.

Compelling "Ask": Your supporters are able to make personal appeals, resonating with potential donors in a way an organization can't.

Extended Reach: You can reach donors otherwise unknown to you by tapping into your supporters' social and family networks. Online social networks are powerful, and your supporters have compelling stories to share. If you can identify your "super social" people, all the better — they will spread your message and deliver support.

Inclusive: Even if volunteers or members are unable to give financially, they can solicit their family and friends to support a cause they feel strongly about.

Compatible with Existing Programs: Peer-to-peer fundraising is supplementary to — not competitive with — your development portfolio. Incorporate it into your current campaigns, and reap the benefits.

Best practices for a successful peer-to-peer fundraising program

Based on quantitative research, qualitative findings, and interviews with leading nonprofits, five best practices emerge:

1. Ensure organization-wide support

2. Encourage or expand online use and eCommunications

3. Provide support

4. Standardize tracking and reporting

5. Create a recognition program

1. Ensure organization-wide support

Nonprofits with organization-wide support for their peer-to-peer programs are more successful. Why? Because when everyone agrees on the value of building partnerships with online constituents, good things happen. Once engaged, peer-to-peer fundraisers can become avid champions and long-term supporters of the organization.

How can you make it work for you?

- Learn who your online fundraisers are — remember, many of them are directly affected by the cause you represent and personify the very audience your mission serves.

- Treat fundraisers like major gift donors, honoring the time, talent, and treasure they give so freely and passionately to your organization.

2. Encourage and expand online use and eCommunications

Ask yourself: Do we have a traditional fundraising channel that could benefit from a complementary online element?

The Salvation Army did just that when they took an offline holiday tradition and added an online program to acquire new donors and appeal to a younger audience. You've probably seen a traditional Red Kettle outside a local retailer, but now everyone has the ability to be a bell ringer via the Online Red Kettle program. Individuals are able to sign up online, create their own Red Kettle and fundraise to support the work of The Salvation

Army. In 2011, online bell ringers raised an additional $1.8 million to support services in 5,000 communities nationwide.

Encouraging peer-to-peer fundraisers to register, communicate, and fundraise online is a win-win situation. Fundraisers can avoid writing receipts, staff can spend less time processing manual offline donations, and the chance of error can be significantly reduced. In practice:

- Set the expectation by requiring everyone to register online.

- Test your website to ensure the registration, donation, and online fundraising tools are intuitive and user friendly. Offering a positive end-user experience is an easy way to encourage repeat usage.

- Communicate the benefits of using online tools and ask your supporters to encourage their supporters to donate online. Benefits include fewer costs to the organization and more time for individuals to fundraise.

3. Provide support

Your supporters are caring, motivated, and asking for guidance. Respond with a support program that educates, empowers, and encourages their participation. They don't want you to run their fundraising program, but they do want assistance and guidance on how they can be successful. Help them marry their passion with your mission:

- Staff a part- or full-time employee (available by phone and email) to provide personal customer service to your peer-to-peer fundraisers.

- Provide materials on that can easily be downloaded. For example:

  - An organization fact sheet

  - A basics of fundraising or hosting an event fact sheet

  - Instructions on how to use online tools

  - Approved logos ("Proud Supporter Of "), letters of support, "Ask," and news release templates

- Stay in touch with all of you peer-to-peer fundraisers, recognizing, and supporting them.

4. Standardize tracking and reporting

Tracking fundraising progress is a crucial step to make sure you're on target to meet your revenue goals. The same rule applies to peer-to-peer fundraising programs. It's important for organizations to standardize reporting to monitor the program's success. Make a list of the standard metrics your organization intends to monitor regularly to measure the program's progress and performance. Consider:

- Number of participants

- Number of repeat versus new participants

- Participant fundraising activity

  - Track the engagement level of participants (number of gifts, emails sent, Facebook messages sent, goals achieved).

  - Proactively communicate with participants regarding their activity levels to encourage them when and where it is needed.

- Number of donors

- Total peer-to-peer online revenue

- Plan on reviewing overall program reports weekly, every other week, or monthly to monitor progress, respond to participant needs, and forecast the future.

5. Create a recognition program

There are three primary reasons a volunteer, participant, or donor gives his or her time, talent, and treasure: To belong, feel good, and be acknowledged. A recognition program is the final element to keep your supporters motivated and committed.

To have an effective recognition program, you don't need to spend money on gifts, but do you do have to be thoughtful about it. Think of it this way: If you give a gift to an organization you feel connected to, how do you want to be recognized?

- Design a recognition program around your objectives.

- Share the successes of top fundraisers and top teams with stories in eNewsletters and on your website.

- Consider offering a "Legacy" or "Super Star" program for long-term and high-achieving peer-to-peer fundraisers.

- Include an "honor roll" on your main page and on participant pages.

- Use social media to celebrate online fundraising efforts, including YouTube, Facebook, and Twitter.

- Include a message board on your website for others to comment and support fundraisers.

- Offer the ability to post tributes allowing fundraisers to share who they are acting in memory of, if appropriate.

Above all

Say "thank you"! Send email or handwritten notes — it's one of the most powerful things you can do! If you follow these best practices, you'll drive revenue, create greater awareness, and acquire new supporters. That is, with a little help from your friends and their friends.

Chapter Two

The Mobile Frontier: Successful Strategies from Text-to-Give and Beyond

by Katya Andresen, Chief Strategy Officer, Network for Good
Tom Krackeler, Former Vice President of Common Ground, Convio

Smartphones, Quick Response Codes, texting. Everywhere you turn there seems to be a new story about mobile, be it on your Facebook page or your local evening news.

Mobile has expanded beyond simple text-to-give campaigns designed to aid in times of emergency. For nonprofits, the magic of mobile is having a way to reach constituents regardless of where they are. Mobile is the most immediate communication channel out there, and there are many proven strategies and emerging techniques for using it to engage your supporters. Fundraise via mobile, allow participants to register for your event, encourage the community to advocate for your cause, or simply use mobile to be accessible and create a dialogue. It's up to you. This chapter provides a brief overview of mobile, outlines its potential benefits, and explores the ways in which your organization can use it for deeper, more personalized engagement. We'll help you ask the right questions to determine if mobile is right for your organization and who should be involved in the effort. And we'll explore ways to successfully integrate mobile into your other fundraising efforts for the most impact.

What does mobile include? Here are the basics:

- Smartphone: A mobile phone built on a computing platform, allowing you to do more than just make calls. Many smartphones such as the Apple iPhone, RIM Blackberry, or those powered by Google's Android software allow you to manage your daily schedule, take photos, check email, and browse the Internet.

- Mobile Web: A browser used to access the Internet via a mobile device. The mobile web poses unique challenges. Because screen sizes are smaller, many organizations streamline the information and work to make sure any site content or forms are easy to use.

- App: If you're familiar with the iPhone, you're familiar with apps, which are small applications that are built to work with smartphones. They do not generally access the mobile web via a browser but instead help the user focus on a specific task — organizing a grocery list, looking up information on a favorite film, booking an airline ticket, etc. Recent research indicates that 35 percent of U.S. adults have cell phones with apps, a number that's expected to continue to grow.[1]

- Text Messaging: Text messaging allows users to exchange brief messages over a network. The messages can be limited to text only or can contain images, video, or sound content and many include a call to action, either to visit a website or respond with a code to make a donation. Text is also among the most popular means of mobile communication with The Pew Research Center reporting that **72 percent of U.S. adult cell phone users send and receive text messages**.

Numbers like 72 percent sound impressive but who's doing the texting? Who's going mobile? In short: Everyone.

Generation Y, defined as the generation of people currently between the ages of 18 and 27 and representing 82 billion consumers, continues to lead the way. Almost 90 percent of users in this age range use their mobile devices to share pictures or blog posts. Additionally, 51 percent of Generation Y in the U.S. report that they use their mobile phone as their primary access to the Internet.[2] According to Convio's research in *The Next Generation of American Giving*, these mobile users aren't just surfing; they're taking action and mobile devices are frequently cited as an emerging channel for Gen Y donors.

But mobile use isn't limited to younger users. Numbers vary, but Nielsen reports more than 1 in 10 adults aged 55 and older are using smartphones.[3] While the numbers are small today compared to younger users, it's important to note that mobile use among baby boomers is growing in surprising ways. Many are using the phones to play games, and tablets like the iPad offer excellent examples of mobile devices that are empowering a broader audience of adults to access and explore the web in new ways. And remember: While this number may seem small, the quality of the boomer audience using mobile devices represents the technology-savvy, often well-educated and affluent who may be good major donor prospects for your organization.

Gen Y: 90% use their mobile devices to share pictures or blog posts.

Boomers: One in ten aged 55 and older are using smartphones.

Civics: 50% were aware of text-to-donate campaigns for Haiti relief.

Gen X: 13% have made donations via text/SMS.

The New Frontier: Text-to-give & beyond

The growing prevalence of mobile in American society, along with the broadening audience for mobile technology like text messaging and apps, is great news for nonprofits. Users from all walks of life are becoming more familiar with mobile as a channel and are willing to engage with the organizations they support from the palms of their hands.

How quickly are nonprofits and donors adapting to the new channel? Mobile giving is already outpacing the historically high adoption rates of online giving. In their recent report, *Real Time Charitable Giving*,[4] the Pew Research Center's Internet & American Life Project discovered that one in five U.S. adults (20 percent) have made a charitable contribution online and that one in ten (9 percent) have made a charitable contribution using the text messaging feature on their mobile phone. That number is rapidly growing.

While standalone mobile campaigns have begun to produce impressive results for their causes, mobile can be even more impactful as part of an integrated campaign because of its ability to provide a relevant, on-demand connection. The mobile web is the most immediate channel available for engaging your audience, providing an "at your fingertips" way for volunteers, donors and supporters to organize their lives, access information and interact daily with the causes they care about most.

Bear in mind that harnessing the power of mobile as a channel — beyond text-to-give campaigns — offers nonprofits other benefits, including the ability to quickly and easily send messages to constituents, giving nonprofits a way to build an opt in database that can be integrated with overall marketing efforts. In other words, mobile is both a great fundraising channel as well as a great way to market to donors and prospects.

Haiti

Prior to January 12, 2010, little more than $1 million had been raised via mobile text; however, in the aftermath of the devastating earthquake in Haiti, close to $50 million was raised via mobile campaigns.

The vast majority of mobile donors (89 percent) heard about the campaign on television and half (50 percent) made their contribution immediately thereafter, for an estimated total of $43 million. This unique phenomenon of "impulse giving" where donors admit to making a spur-of-the-moment contribution without much additional research has since extended to other natural disasters including fundraising to assist in the cleanup of the U.S. Gulf Coast following the BP oil spill and the March 2011 tsunami and earthquake in Japan.

With the success of mobile fundraising efforts for the Haiti earthquake and Japan tsunami in mind, many nonprofits look to micro-donations via mobile to support their fundraising efforts. However, for many organizations, the economics of text-to-give may not make sense without forging a partnership with phone companies and the sheer marketing muscle necessary to make most text campaigns a success.

American Red Cross Text-to-Give Haiti Disaster Relief Campaign:

- Text 90999 to donate $10

- 100% of donations went to Red Cross

- $800K raised in 24 hours

- $5 million raised via mobile by day 26

Mobile as a channel

Ready to think outside the box? Consider the following alternatives:

Text message ticklers

Let's say you work for an animal welfare organization. While you'd like to raise funds via mobile, it's not the right time yet — there's not an emergency in your community and you're reluctant to risk donor fatigue by using mobile to fundraise for your big yearly ask. According to recent research,[5] 85 percent of people read an unread text message within 15 minutes of receiving one — providing a great click-through rate and, in some cases, a click-through rate superior to what can be accomplished with email. Why not use text messaging to share some fun facts and successes about your organization? By sending just a couple of text messages per month, you can keep potential donors excited about your cause and keep your organization top of mind with supporters.

Gateway to the telephone

Interested in moving donors up the giving ladder? Mobile may be a great place to start. Doctors without Borders, an Australian-based organization, partnered with a local carrier to send text messages to wireless customers asking if they could be contacted by telephone to contribute funds for Asian tsunami relief.[6] Sixty percent of SMS recipients opted to participate in the monthly solicitation with an impressive 50 percent subsequently choosing to enroll in the organization's monthly giving plan. While it may be difficult to navigate the ground rules around proactive outreach via text, using it as an "opt in" for more personal means of communication may offer a new approach, particularly for organizations responding to crisis.

The sweet ring of success

Mobile engagement extends beyond the text message — look for ways to harness media and entertainment content. For example, special ringtones can provide a unique and audible call to action reminding donors frequently of your cause and/or providing an opportunity to share your story with friends, family, and coworkers. A children's arts organization could provide a brief clip from a performance while an environmental organization may look to sounds from unfamiliar species to pique the interest of passersby. For example, the Marine Mammal Center offers ringtones for the Pacific Harbor seal, the Steller sea lion, and humpback whale songs at no charge.

Engage them on-the-go

Simple calls to action work best for the mobile constituent. For instance, you could provide a mobile-optimized form to encourage them to donate or participate in a petition or other campaign component. If you're a community organization, how about asking supporters to photograph and report activities in their local neighborhood using Facebook, Twitter, or other mobile-enabled social media? In your call to action, focus on one or two key actions and prioritize them so that one is clearly at the forefront.

If you're giving away an asset such as a tip sheet, reference guide, or top-ten list, make sure it's easy for your mobile constituent to download, digest, and share. Share tips and easy-to-reference information on a variety of topics, from safe-to-eat seafood, to 16 seasonal suggestions to support a caregiver, or even a visual guide to local poisonous plants!

Empower your organization

Mobile is more than a powerful channel to engage supporters; it can transform your organization's development office and beyond if you know how to use the tools available. Think about a board meeting with major gift prospects for a Sunday brunch — why not give board members the power to log conversation information or understand the relationship between this prospect and others while waiting in the restaurant's parking lot? CRM systems make this possible through easy-to-use mobile access. Coming from a successful meeting? You don't need to be at your desk to start running with the ideas that resulted — use your mobile device to assign tasks to various members of your staff to keep the positive momentum going. Or, while you're out delivering programs in the community, use your mobile device to track client progress in your CRM and share the exciting news through social media.

Is mobile right for you?

So you're thinking about adding mobile to your outreach strategy. How do you determine if it's right for your organization?

The best way to ask yourself if mobile is right for your organization is to ask if mobile is right for your audience. Mobile is no different from other forms of marketing and fundraising in that good strategy starts with your audience and works backwards from there, rather than starting with your organization and thinking of audience at the end of your planning process.

So with that mindset, let's explore mobile potential for your audience. Here are a few strategic questions to lead you to the right answers about whether to pursue a mobile program.

1.   Who are your constituents and what are they like?

Mobile is all about reaching the right people, in the right place, at the right time. First, think about your audience and where, when, and how you interact with these people.

Think about the segment of people that you are hoping to reach with mobile. What are their ages? They most certainly own mobile devices, but how do they use them? Current mobile donors tend to skew slightly younger and are more tech-savvy than average donors. If your constituencies are older and don't have smartphones, it's important to come to terms with that — though mobile still may make sense if you're trying to reach a new group of supporters beyond your current base.

Now consider why and how this audience typically chooses to support you. What is the driving concern that binds people to your cause? Which types of appeals are they most inclined to answer (legislative alerts, time-sensitive campaigns, end-of-year appeals)? What times that you interact with them are conducive to inspiring action via mobile (for example, a walk or gala or volunteer day, when staff interact with individuals interested in learning more about your organization, or when your supporters are checking email on their smartphones)? —

2.   What resources do you have to commit to mobile?

Before delving into the exciting possibilities mobile has to offer, it's important to do a reality check. What investment can you afford to make in mobile? Take a moment to consider what resources you have in the way of:

- Time
- Expertise
- Money
- Staff

In considering your staff, ask yourself who needs to be involved at each stage of mobile, especially in the beginning. Who needs to be involved in the decision to embark on mobile? Who will be engaged in implementation? The staff who are typically included in mobile decisions and implementation include: the executive director; technology, marketing, and communications department members; program managers; development professionals; and advocacy professionals.

Ideally, you'll want to include those people in your discussions of the questions we pose here and the planning process that we recommend.

The more collaboration you have at the start, the more likely you are to win and keep internal support and end up with a successful program.

What do you want to want the audience to do? What are your goals with this audience? Are you trying to use mobile to:

- Increase engagement levels?
- Recruit volunteers?
- Increase donations?
- Transmit information?
- Reduce costs?
- Receive information?
- Increase advocacy?

Given those goals, ask yourself what actions make sense. Do you want your audience to:

- Donate via text?
- Pledge to donate later?
- Donate on a mobile page?
- Sign a petition?
- Set up a recurring gift?
- Answer a poll?
- Give by voice?
- Get important information?
- Spread the word via social networks?
- Report a problem or something praiseworthy in their community?

3. How will this fit into your other outreach efforts?

You have lots of ideas about mobile; now we need to step back and look at mobile in the bigger picture. Your mobile strategy should not exist in isolation. It's important that you use mobile to supplement, reinforce, and enhance your other forms of outreach. Mobile isn't a separate activity, it's an integrated part of acquisition, fundraising, cultivation, and marketing activities. Think about both how you will leverage existing outreach to build mobile presence and drive results in other forms of outreach. For example:

- Online and Offline Donations: Think about collecting phone numbers and asking people to opt in for mobile alerts.

- Donor Acknowledgement: Consider mentioning mobile in your donor receipts or welcome packets and inviting people to opt in — or sending thank you texts to monthly donors via mobile.

- Emergencies: When you email outreach for disaster relief or other time-sensitive emergencies or special bulletins, consider including a mobile-friendly page link or text-to-give code since so many people check mail on their phone, and consider links to critical updates

- Special Events: At special events, invite people at check-in to opt in to mobile. Think about how you can enhance the event experience by asking people to text to donate or sign up for email or visit a mobile-friendly page where they can take some form of action.

- Campaigns: Consider launching campaigns via mobile and following up with direct mail or email appeals (or vice versa).

- Social Media: Since many mobile givers are active in social media, it's important to integrate mobile and social outreach. Make it easy for mobile users to spread the word via social media, and include mobile opt ins in social media content.

- Education: Think about how mobile can help you disseminate information more effectively — for example, with a daily tip on pet care or managing your diabetes or an app for finding a nearby YMCA.

- General Outreach: Make sure any mobile information about your cause is included on everything, from annual reports to newsletters to press releases. You could invite people to text a short code to opt in for mobile updates or emails.

4. How are you going to measure your efforts?

Now let's turn to how to measure success in mobile marketing. You'll need to look at two things — your return on investment and your return on engagement. For example:

Return on Investment:

- Cost savings (Did mobile help you gain more efficiency? Use less staff time? Consume less paper?)

- Donations from mobile or added donations or purchases from other forms of outreach that will be driven by mobile reinforcement (better online giving results, better direct mail results, more event attendance)

Return on Engagement:

- New supporters (who may not yet be giving)

- Added convenience/immediacy for supporters in order to build loyalty to your cause

- Improved advocacy results

- Brand exposure, including whether constituents who receive and engage with your mobile programs contribute, volunteer, and advocate at a higher level than those who just receive mail or visit your website

Making mobile happen

Now that you've asked yourself all sorts of soul-searching questions about mobile — hopefully with key colleagues — you have a checklist of the considerations you need for a go/no-go decision on mobile. If mobile looks like the right choice for your organization, your next step will be to choose the right mobile solution and create a plan for implementing it.

Take the time to clarify some of the things you're looking for to help narrow your options and articulate what you're looking for in potential donors:

- Define your audience, desired actions, and goals/objectives.

- Assess the resources you will commit and the anticipated return on investment (or return on engagement).

- Collaborate with key members of your team on planning and design of the program.

- Identify how you will deliver, promote, and support your mobile efforts.

- Measure and analyze your mobile program.

- Ensure your existing outreach and engagement systems are prepared for the introduction of your mobile program.

Next, it's time to evaluate potential solution providers. There are two main questions to keep in mind:

Question 1: What type of vendor do you want?

Mobile technology vendors come in all shapes and sizes. Some specialize in particular solutions, while others focus exclusively on nonprofit organizations, while still more can provide a complete solution where mobile is just one piece of a much larger system.

Think about what type of mobile capabilities you need to create the constituent experience you're seeking. Is it event registration? The ability to make donations on the go? Multimedia offerings like free ringtones or an app? Are you only interested in mobile functionality for your staff so they can make real-time updates to a donor record or assign tasks from the road?

Question 2: How will you qualify your vendor?

You've got a short list of people whose work you admire — maybe you encountered them online, found out about them from a board member, or met them at a local trade show. Whether you're searching for a fully integrated solution or for support to help your in-house IT team, be sure to consider the following:

- Industry leadership. Make sure the vendor has experience meeting the unique needs of nonprofit organizations and understands the challenges of marketing messages to donors, supporters, and volunteers specifically.

- Expertise. Confirm that the vendor has experience launching the kind of mobile programs you're interested in, along with analytics, strategy, creative, and launch.

- Disaster recovery. What happens if the server crashes? What if there's high traffic from a matching gift opportunity and you want to send a text alert to constituents or create a mobile form on the fly? Asking about stability can be particularly helpful if you're evaluating a cloud-based mobile solution for your team versus one that's web-hosted or installed on computers in your offices. Ask how quickly it can get back into service. If they're industry leaders, they'll have automatically secured your information and you won't even notice the downtime.

- Pricing. You often get what you pay for. Make sure that the product and/or service you're purchasing includes key attributes that will make you successful like support, training and ongoing development to keep your mobile investment ahead of the curve.

Making the most of your mobile channel is similar, in many ways, to engaging your constituents online. Whomever you chose as a partner has to be at the top of their game and able to keep up to date with marketing technologies and capabilities that are evolving rapidly. The right mobile partner has a broad set of capabilities combined with a deep understanding of each primary mobile channel. A vendor with a breadth of capabilities, in mobile and beyond, ensures that your organization's technology not only works well, but helps you achieve your desired end result and is a pleasure for anyone on your staff to use.

1   The Rise of Apps Culture, Pew Internet & American Life Project and Nielsen, http://
    pewinternet.org/~/media//Files/Reports/2010/PIP_Nielsen%20Apps%20Report.pdf
2   State of the Mobile Web, Opera http://www.opera.com/smw/2010/10/
3   Who is Winning the Smartphone Battle, Nielsen http://blog.nielsen.com/nielsenwire/
    online_mobile/who-is-winning-the-u-s-smartphone-battle/
4   Real Time Charitable Giving, Pew Internet & American Life Project and The Berkman
    Center for Internet & Society at Harvard University. http://www.pewinternet.org

Chapter Three

Understanding the Value of Your Social Media Influencers: How to Identify and Empower Those Who Can Engage an Entire Community

by Danielle Brigida, Manager of Social Media, National Wildlife Federation
Mark Davis, Director of Enterprise Internet Solutions, Blackbaud
Casey Golden, Chief Executive Officer, Small Act

Ever since the March for Lesbian and Gay Rights on October 11, 1987, thousands of LGBT people and allies celebrate October 11 as National Coming Out Day (NCOD). In 2010, the Human Rights Campaign (HRC) recognized that NCOD needed a 21st century renovation and turned its attention to social media. Through the creation of their "Coming Out for Equality" Facebook app, HRC empowered thousands of LGBT supporters; as a result, 125,000 people donated their Facebook status for equality, 6,000+ tweets for equality were sent, and 117,000 new email addresses were added to HRC's database. By expanding their social network, HRC built an army that was ready to fight when the Marriage Equality Bill was up for vote. HRC constituents voiced their support through 460,000 election-related action alert emails, 51 celebrity videos, 47,199 emails to state lawmakers, and more. Their actions, through traditional channels and social media, were pivotal in the passing of New York's Marriage Equality Act on June 24, 2011.

The question today is not whether you should use social media, but how you should use the information your constituents are sharing on social media to attract more people to your mission and make your fundraising campaigns more successful. It is a question on every manager's mind as people flock to social media sites in astounding numbers and as social media users influence attitudes about everything from television shows and political campaigns to energy drinks and causes to support. The answer to the question lies in understanding your social media constituents and identifying which ones are the most "social"— those who best interact with and influence others across their online networks — because, while each of your constituents is a potential donor, some are more adept at spreading the word and energizing others. By knowing these active, influential social media constituents, you are in a position to develop mutually beneficial relationships with them that respects their advocacy for your cause.

Consumers trust online friends over advertisers

According to a 2011 Nielsen study of online consumers, 92 percent of those surveyed trust recommendations by friends, family, and word of mouth above all other forms of advertising, and 70 percent of consumers trust online consumer reviews by people they don't know.[1] Additionally, research by NM Incite found that three out of five — a full 60 percent — of social media users write product and service reviews, and that 63 percent of users choose consumer ratings as their preferred source of information about products and services.[2]

This is compelling information when combined with the fact that the majority of adults in America who are online use social networking sites.[3] It also shines a light on the fact that organizations no longer drive one-way conversations. Through social media, people have a channel to instantly share their opinions with hundreds, sometimes thousands, of others. Information has never spread so fast and with so much power to affect brands and products. Faced with these new realities, social media-savvy nonprofits are working to better understand their social media constituents and form deeper connections with them.

Who's social?

The best way to understand the social media users among your constituents is to use a social media data enrichment service to analyze your database and assign each of your constituents a "social score," a number that represents the breadth, depth, frequency, and scale of his or her social media interactions. In other words, the social score is a measurement of a constituent's connectivity with others through their social networks. Based on that number, individuals can be segmented into one of four categories: Key Influencer, Engager, Multichannel Consumer, or Standard Consumer. Each group plays a different role on social media networks, and each one of them is important to your organization's success.

How social media constituents help deliver your mission

Each of the four social media categories has unique characteristics and its members relate to each other and to your campaigns in different ways.

Key Influencers champion your cause

These are the "super social" people at the top of your social media pyramid; although they account for only one percent of your social media constituents, they are highly engaged and capable of influencing not only the people they know but also social media members they don't know. When they interact with others, they have a powerful impact. Their posts are widely read and shared by more people than posts generated by any other group. They belong to the top three major social networks — Facebook, Twitter, and LinkedIn — and are the few that deliver messages to the many. Think of them as citizen journalists, those who write for a mass market.

Engagers drive your messages

Social media Engagers are dialed into what is happening in the social media space and create and deliver new content. If they relate to news from a trusted Key Influencer, they will rapidly retweet, redistribute, and relay information. They will help your compelling stories go viral. They will increase awareness of your organization and expand your constituency. Through them, you can reach more people who are likely to support you because someone they trust has given your organization his or her stamp of approval. Engagers make good social chairs and members of executive committees for local events, and they may form a deep commitment to your organization.

These people belong to all three major networks, and although only about five percent of all social media users fall into this category, they drive up to 80 percent of content and communications. They are your broadcasters: They generate posts, share information, virally spread messages, and collaborate with others. They have well-established social networks and have earned the trust of their groups. They are strong influencers of people they know personally.

Multichannel and Standard Consumers respect the opinions of Key Influencers and Engagers

Your Multichannel Consumers are active on at least two social network sites; multichannel consumers make up about 39 percent of all social media users. They enjoy keeping up with social media content and occasionally participate. They influence to some extent — via normal friend-to-friend engagement and passing along information to their networks — but due to their level of activity, their sphere of influence is not a dominant part of their persona.

Standard Consumers typically belong to one social network to keep up with friends, family, and current events. While they read and watch updates more than they create new content or make comments, they are influenced by their more socially active friends and family. As a group, they account for 55 percent of all social media users.

Connect with and empower your social media users

Following are some recommendations of how best to involve each of the social media groups in your mission.

Key Influencers: Treat them as citizen journalists and they will help you shape and guide public discussions on social networks.

Get to know them in a mid- to high-touch relationship. While they are less likely to make big financial contributions, they care about you and influence the gifts of others. Find out what is important to them and why they relate to your organization — what is in it for them, if you will. Do some research to find out why they support you. Are they interested in protecting endangered species? Does a family member have a disease you are trying to cure? Have they successfully graduated from your institution? By looking at the information they post online, you may be able to understand how to engage them, because once you know that, the level of engagement will be significantly higher.

Provide them with early access to information, announcements, and special events.

- Connect with them both in social and traditional means to enhance the fullness and depth of the relationship.

- Provide them compelling, bite-size content that is easy for them to distribute, share, and discuss on your behalf.

Engagers: Find out who they are and what they care about, so you can get closer to them. They will help you keep your social community alive.

- Start categorizing their interests and passions to use in future campaigns and calls to action that match what they care about most.

- Design mid- to low-barrier calls to action for those who are not yet actively engaged with you. These should not simply ask them to "like" your page, but encourage them to share their opinions and voices on your page — something that encourages them to articulate why your organization is important to them. This could be in the form of a survey, a question, or a request to post about a photo or comment about himself or herself.

Multichannel Consumers: Target them with online and offline campaigns.

- Create low-barrier opportunities to increase their connection with your brand on the social networks by soliciting feedback, votes, or personal stories. This connection will create a constant path of information flow to this group even though their action rate on the social networks will be moderate.

- Involve them in campaigns that have cross-channel opportunities to take action. For example:
  - Online campaigns that include a link to volunteer opportunities
  - Offline campaigns that allow them to read current stories and get involved on Facebook or Twitter

Standard Consumers: This group also needs very low barrier opportunities to increase their connection to your mission, but a personal experience with you or supporting someone they know with a fundraising donation will more likely be successful.

- Use the same approach to online and offline campaigns as you would with multichannel consumers with a focus on Facebook, their preferred network.

Using social scores to increase event fundraising

Encouraging event participation and online fundraising are natural fits for your Key Influencers and Engagers as research shows that those who score high on social media interactions are better peer-to-peer fundraisers than those who don't. A 2011 Blackbaud study also found that peer-to-peer fundraisers increased fundraising by 40 percent by using their social networks over years when they didn't.[4] Their ability to raise funds comes from their social networks. Make sure you give them event information early. To forge a strong connection, you could invite them to a pre-event meeting, a webinar, or a conference call so they have unique information and content to discuss.

The American Cancer Society is planning to put this concept to the test by using social scores to target recipients of their half-marathon, marathon, and triathlon direct marketing appeals. By analyzing email addresses, the organization has been able to identify constituents who are: interested in running, have high interaction ratings on social media sites, and have made a donation to the organization in the past 24 months — now that is a target audience! Ensuring these runners have information about the events that is engaging and easy to distribute to their social networks will be key.

Social scores target social supporters

The National Wildlife Federation, a nonprofit that works to inspire Americans to protect wildlife for our children's future, has recently studied the social media behaviors of its members and donors through database analysis, social scoring, and publicly available social media information. Their goal is to acquire a more complete picture of constituent interactions with the organization so they can make strategic decisions about where to allocate outreach resources.

First, they used publicly available social media information and mixed it with past constituent interactions from various platforms, allowing them to get a clearer picture of their supporters than they had ever had before. Then, by mixing how they interact with these constituents on social platforms, they are able to see supporters as individuals rather than simple names or addresses and work with them to leverage their social influence.

One way the National Wildlife Federation uses social scoring to reach out to a wider audience is to connect with people who have participated in past events and who could be doing more to spread the organization's message on social media. For example, in looking at data, staff members discovered that people who participate in the organization's annual Great American Backyard Campout have higher than average social scores. This is an important piece of information, and staff members decided that strategic outreach to this group will make a difference in realizing its mission of connecting children with nature — social people share more and influence others.

The Federation also finds great value in having access to social history as well as participant data, because it allows them to spend less time researching and more time connecting with constituents in the ways they want to be talked to. By targeting a specific region and people in that region who score at the Engager level or higher, they plan to test how well-targeted outreach increases event participation and results in social supporters spreading the organization's message. Like many nonprofits, the National Wildlife Federation does not have a lot of time or money on spend on outreach, which it is why it is so important for them to know their supporters' social strengths and how they can empower them to spread the word on important issues. That's because supporters who authentically spread your message over social media channels influence many others.

Conclusion

Social media offers a wealth of publicly available information to help you better understand your constituents. By segmenting them through social scores, you are able to identify those highly connected individuals who encourage and influence others with content, product, and service reviews, and endorsements. With this information, you can get to know those individuals, collaborate with them, and use their social skills to advocate for your organization. A clear view of your social media constituents is critical as people increasingly rely on each other to endorse, defend and decry products and causes.

1. Nielsen: Global Consumers' Trust in 'Earned' Advertising Grows in Importance, April 10, 2012
2. Neilson and NM Incite, State of the Media: The Social Media Report, Q3 2011.
3. Pew Internet & American Life Project, August 26, 2011. Accessed on March 23, 2012, http://pewinternet.org/Reports/2011/Social-Networking-Sites/Overview.aspx
4. Blackbaud. 2011

Chapter Four

Principal Giving:
The Race Is On for Transformational Donors

by Melissa Bank Stepno, Target Analytics Senior Consultant, Blackbaud

Principal, transformational, and lead gifts are critically important — without them, you cannot expect to secure and sustain your mission. For many years, nonprofits have tracked with the 80/20 rule. That is, an organization could expect to receive 80 percent of its funding from 20 percent of its donors. In recent years, however, many organizations have seen this ratio shift to 95/5 or even 97/3. This dramatic change is due to a combination of shifting wealth, a weakening economy, and the changing priorities of funders. Today, many organizations find that their best donors have suffered losses in liquidity during the recent recession and/or are feeling "tapped out" by the nonprofits they have supported heavily in the past. Maintaining your competitive edge by cultivating new principal gift donors will prove transformational for your organization. It's a commitment that has to come from the very top of the organization and be reflected in all of your systems and processes.

On your mark: Set the stage

Principal giving strategies encourage those with extraordinary resources to make an extraordinary impact. Typically, a principal gift is one that far exceeds an organization's entry point for major giving and is designed to distinguish the extraordinary donors from the significant donors. It's a distinction that varies from organization to organization. Principal giving can start at $100,000, $1 million, $5 million, or even $10 million. There's no clear rule; if your organization considers $1,000 to be a major gift, your organization may define principal gifts starting at the $100,000 level, whereas an organization whose major giving level starts at $100,000 may consider $5 million to be a principal gift.

But, it's not the dollar value that matters. It's the commitment you, as an organization, make to differentiating your approach to working with principal gift prospects. While it's well accepted that major giving prospects require higher-touch cultivation and relationship building than typical annual fund and lower dollar donors, with principal gift prospects relationship building is paramount.

As organizations continue to up the ante with more and more aggressive campaign goals, they have increasingly high expectations to meet. Consider that when the 80/20 rule held true, the one billion dollar campaign was virtually non-existent. Now, campaigns this size and larger are becoming commonplace at premier institutions. And as organizations become more aggressive in their fundraising goals, they will find fewer prospects able and willing to support the apex of their fundraising campaigns. For example, one large research university expects 11 donors to fund 80 percent of the campaign they are about to launch. To be successful, the expectation is that this will all have to be in the form of principal gifts that require organization-wide focus.

According to a study by The Spectrem Group, there are 8.6 million households in the U.S. with a net worth (excluding primary residence) of at least $1 million.[1] The number of households with at least $5 million in assets reduces this to just 1 million, and, at the $25 million level, the U.S. has 107,000 households. This may seem like a lot of households but compared with charitable needs and translated to charitable dollars, you'll see that you're looking at a very small group of individuals who are capable of making an extraordinary principal gift.

This point is reinforced by a 2010 study, High Net Worth Philanthropy, sponsored by Bank of America Merrill Lynch and written by The Center on Philanthropy at Indiana University.[2] It surveyed high-net worth individuals who either have an annual household income of $200,000 or more or have a net worth (excluding primary residence) of at least $1 million. Researchers found that among these groups, the biggest motivator for charitable giving was being "moved at how [their] gift can make a difference." They also found that although almost every respondent made charitable contributions, most gifts were relatively low. In 2009, only 10.5 percent of the study's respondents gave a total of $100,000 or more to nonprofits – and that was total giving, not to one specific organization. Couple this with the fact that $100,000 is the lowest level generally seen for principal giving to an organization and you see how few principal gift prospects truly exist.

So, what can be learned from the research? First, principal giving cannot simply be about finding wealthy people in an organization's database — it takes a more sophisticated look at donors and focuses on finding the right combination of factors including the:

- Right donor

- Right purpose

- Right amount

- Right solicitor

- Right time

A 2011 study by Dini Partners[3] of donors who contributed $100,000 to $1 million found that the single most important factor influencing giving is alignment with an organization's mission. And, when choosing new programs to support, more than 50 percent of donors surveyed cited a personal relationship to an organization or cause as the most important factor in choosing to support it.

Wise philanthropists reinforce this concept time and time again by affirming, "It's about fundraising, friend-raising, and matchmaking." It's about: "giving a person an opportunity to support a good cause." It's about: "matching the right person to the right projects." In formal studies and casual conversation philanthropists are clear: "It's about building relationships, not about the money."

Get set: Identify the right prospects

To effectively find this right combination in a donor, start at the beginning with proper prospect identification. This occurs long before cultivation and relationship building come into play.

Identifying Need

To identify the right prospects for your organization, you have to understand your organization's needs, your case for support. This is a crucial step when you embark on the task of identifying new prospects, especially for principal giving. Typically, nonprofits tend to focus only on past giving and perceived wealth, but to be successful, it's worth employing a more sophisticated and educated approach. Ask yourself the following:

- What are your organization's top funding initiatives?

- Why are they the most important?

- When will funding for these initiatives be needed?

- How much funding is needed for each one?

- What additional initiatives are coming down the road?

- How do these initiatives help your organization fulfill its mission?

- Why are these initiatives compelling and unique to your organization?

- Is your "organizational house" in order?

If you can't answer these questions, step back and do your homework first. If you're confident in your answers, it's time to begin identifying the appropriate principal gift prospects for your organization.

Identifying Capacity and Inclination

Who in your database has both the wealth (capacity) to fund your initiatives and the inclination (likelihood, desire, affinity) to do so? This is called the "sweet spot," because it requires your potential donors to show both capacity and inclination. The reality is, your biggest champions may not have the wealth to fund your initiatives at the principal gift level, and the wealthiest potential donors may have no interest in your initiatives.

A good way to find the sweet spot of capacity and inclination is to use predictive modeling—the process by which a model, or profile, of those who have already done what you're measuring is created, enabling you to find others who look like the model.

Today, by pooling principal-level donors together and examining millions of distinct datasets and giving patterns, it's possible to develop a "profile model" of the ideal principal gift prospect. The profile includes information specific to both a prospect's relationship to your organization and more generally to the prospect's capacity, wealth, and philanthropic interest so you know you're hitting that sweet spot.

So What Makes a Principal Gift Prospect?

One thing you should look for in a principal gift prospect is general philanthropic propensity. Our research shows that donors who show loyalty to an organization through consistent giving provide the base of prospects with potential for increased commitment. This is supported by traditional fundraising theory, which states that those who have given to an organization in the past are more likely to give to the organization in the future. Or, in industry lingo, retention is more successful than acquisition. For example, one client shared that their year-over-year retention rate is about 80 percent while their new donor acquisition rate is one percent. Similarly, in benchmarking 10 large nonprofits, we found a correlation between raising more dollars through the organization's major giving program and the average length of time a donor was affiliated with the organization prior to making their first major gift.

However, there is much more to the picture than being philanthropic to your organization. Principal gift prospects typically have high incomes, are well educated, and enjoy a comfortable lifestyle, belonging to affluent demographic groups and living in expensive homes situated in communities with a high quality of life. In addition to income, their community, and the value of their residence, their other assets are higher than the norm as well.

Capacity

Remember, just because donors have the inclination to support your mission, they cannot be principal gift prospects if they don't have the capacity to do so. And, while our research indicates that having a certain threshold of high income is one factor in being indicative of principal giving, there are many high income earners that are overextended or not interested in making principal gifts. So, a deeper dive into a donor's actual circumstances is necessary to fully vet potential capacity. Whether or not you're using a predictive model, you should use a combination of an electronic wealth screening and a research review. Screenings will help lead you in the right direction, but a screening's limited view of publicly-searchable databases typically only — cleanly and easily — uncovers 20 to 40 percent of a person's wealth. This is why research is needed; it allows you to get "into the weeds" and dive deeper, to better understand the data through more comprehensive analysis and investigation.

Having said that, true capacity may not be determined until a personal relationship with the prospect is cultivated. Through personal relationships, you'll not only be able to uncover additional wealth (is that a real Monet hanging in the hallway?), but you'll also be able to better understand potential liabilities (so, all five children are currently attending a pricey private school?). Significant wealth will not enable a principal gift if encumbrances are equally high. And, behind-the-desk research alone will not unearth all pertinent information.

Inclination

Inclination to give can be a bit more difficult to determine. Typically, you can start to make an assessment of an individual's inclination by answering these questions:

- What is the prospect's relationship with your organization? This includes past giving, advocacy, event participation, constituency, and anything else that connects them to you.

- Where else has the prospect given, and at what level?

- Does the prospect sit on any philanthropic or foundation boards?

- What is the prospect's motivation for giving?

- Are there personal circumstances that may mitigate or strengthen their perceived interest in your organization?

- Who else might they know at your organization (staff, board, volunteers) that could help answer these questions, and importantly, help build a relationship between your organization and this prospect?

The cultivation process is designed, in part, to help explore someone's specific inclination in more detail. But, if you cannot find positive answers to some of these questions upfront, and if you're only looking at someone because of their perceived capacity, it might be time to move on. Always remember, to find the right prospect, you have to look for the sweet spot.

Go: Be operational ready

Are you ready to start identifying principal gift prospects? Not so fast! Principal giving is not just about adding a new level to your development pyramid or understanding your organization's needs or finding the right prospects. In many ways, principal giving is a mindset, a paradigm shift, a different way of approaching development work. You have to be ready to enter the race.

To assess your organizational readiness, you must already have a major gifts program and a dedicated major gifts team in place. Principal giving is not the place to start your high-touch cultivation-based fundraising program. It's a top-drawer add-on — something to consider when, and only when, you already have a good system in place and a culture of major giving firmly established.

Buy-in from the top is critical

- First, your chief development officer has to be onboard with shifting some of your team's efforts to a higher degree of fundraising. Immediate ROI may not be evident, but secured principal gifts can help provide transformational funding for your organization. It's similar to investing in a planned giving program: The rewards may take a while to realize, but once they are, they can alter the future of an organization.

- Second, your chief development officer has to advocate for a principal giving program to your CEO, President, and Board. This is necessary because your principal gift prospects will frequently (and rightly so) expect them to be involved in the process of cultivation and solicitation. In many cases, while it may still fall to the development professional to make the actual "ask," principal giving prospects will expect your organization's leaders to be at the table.

- Finally, all of your organization's director-level stakeholders should also be involved (at colleges, this is typically academic deans; at hospitals, chief medical staff; at service agencies, program directors). These individuals know better than anyone how to best identify and articulate your case for support. They are also often better able to articulate passion for your mission in a way that comes across as more genuine than the development professional can.

Ready your development team and systems

Dedicated frontline gift officers are a must to ensure you have the appropriate resources needed to build close relationships with principal gift prospects. If major giving is high-touch, principal giving is ultra-high touch. Typically, principal gift prospects require more personal contacts with your organization. Someone needs to both develop and orchestrate this relationship. Additionally you need:

- A prospect management system with a staff member responsible for oversight: Given the intensity of principal giving, a prospect management system will ensure that prospects are being identified and moved to qualification, cultivation, and solicitation stages in a timely manner. Having a person who is not only responsible for the relationship with the prospect but also responsible for the process itself will help assure productivity across your team. Keeping a critical eye on solicitation plans, activity/inactivity, and gift officer case loads are all important aspects. In fact, in many cases, organizations will find that gift officers working with principal giving typically see their portfolio size reduced specifically so attention can be better focused on a few key prospects.

- A researcher or researchers to provide the in-depth information, synthesis, and analysis needed for understanding your principal gift prospects: Ideally, the researcher should not just be tasked with identification, they should also partner with your gift officers, becoming a part of the strategy process needed to help build a relationship with a prospect.

- A strong constituent relationship management (CRM) system that allows you to track all activity related to your prospects in one centralized place: And, this means everything — every internal strategy decision, personalized touch-point, mailing, gift receipt, event attended — that can help your organization get a 360-degree view of the prospect and your organization. It may seem like overkill, or administrative hassle, but keep in mind that you're building a relationship between an extraordinary prospect and an organization;

your team is a conduit for the relationship itself. Staff members come and go; the hope is that your prospect's relationship with your organization will endure. Therefore, detailed record keeping, and the building of your organization's institutional memory, will be crucial in keeping processes organized and the relationship forward-moving.

Everything ready? Move to the starting block!

To realize a successful principal giving program, an organization has to be prepared to go the distance. Like running a successful marathon, principal giving is epitomized by the planning and process that is put in place, only here the goal is not to cross the finish line but to help guide extraordinary prospects toward providing extraordinary gifts. Ultimately, "It's about building relationships, not about the money." And, identifying prospective donors with the right sweet spot must be at the beginning of creating a true partnership. It is through these partnerships that you have the potential to transform your organization and achieve your mission.

1. Affluent Market Insights 2012 report, Spectrem Group, March 21, 2012, http://www. spectrem.com/content/spectrem-group-release-3-21-12
2. 2010 Study of High Net Worth Philanthropy, Bank of America, Merrill Lynch, November 2010, http://www.philanthropy.iupui.edu/Research/docs/2010BAML_ HighNetWorthPhilanthropy.pdf
3. Giving in 2011, Dini Partners: http://www.dinipartners.com/UserFiles/File/2011_Non-Profit_Giving_Survey.pdf

Chapter Five

Analyzing the Value of Special Events: Strategies for Success

by Susan Ulrich McLaughlin, CFRE, Principal Consultant, Blackbaud

If you're involved in special event fundraising, you know there's never a shortage of ideas. We have all been at the conference room table when a well-meaning volunteer or board member suggests that we try a new event to raise funds. The suggestion is usually prefaced with, "I recently went to an event that ..." or "A local nonprofit had success with..."

But, before agreeing to try something that seemed to work for someone else, you need to consider whether your organization needs or can afford another special event, because while events have a place in every fundraising program, the goals and objectives of each event must be evaluated. It's easy to get consumed with the details of staging an event — booking a venue, promoting the event, creating seating charts, choosing a menu — and forget the most important objective is to acquire supporters.

Recently, I took an informal survey of nonprofits, asking how the economy has affected overall fundraising performance. Results showed that the biggest impact of the economic downturn was decreased revenue and participation at events. Not much of a surprise: In a tough economy, budgets get tighter and expendable items such as benefit golf tournaments and galas are either cut from the budget or downsized. Businesses and individuals consider special events to be a luxury, not a necessity.

In the same vein, nonprofits should consider special events to be a luxury and not a necessity. No organization should rely on net proceeds from special events as a primary funding source. And given that belief, you will find that without the pressure of staging event after event to meet revenue goals, you can truly analyze the value of your special events.

"Friend-raising" events

Your organization may use the term "friend-raiser" to describe events and, in fact, every special event is a friendraiser. Events provide the opportunity to raise awareness and engage new constituents, as well as raise money. However, this philosophy only works when there is a plan in place to continue to engage newfound friends after the event. All too often, after the dollars are counted and thank-you notes sent, staff members have to focus on the next event without having time to engage with the "friends" they just raised.

It's a significant oversight: By ignoring new donors until the next year when it's time to start planning for the same event, opportunity is lost.

Avoid this problem by identifying your goals and objectives in advance of each event, allowing you to develop a strategy of qualification and cultivation of any new friends. This will not only add to the value of your event, it will add to the overall fundraising success of your organization.

Defining goals and objectives

A special event should not be owned by one person, but should engage many people including the nonprofit's CEO, CDO, major gift officers, prospect researchers, volunteers, and board members. Collaboration is critical to maximizing the value of your event.

Converting a new friend to a major gift donor requires you to implement a strategy well before the date of the event. Invite your key stakeholders to your first event-planning meeting — your leadership team has to be present and engaged to help set overall goals and objectives and to take ownership of specific tasks. And speaking of goals — every event should consider metrics that include:

Number of:

- New attendees, returning attendees

- New sponsorships, renewed sponsorships, upgraded sponsorships

- Donations only

Amount from:

- New sponsorships, renewed sponsorships, upgraded sponsorships

- New attendees, returning attendees

- From donations only

With your goals set, look at your objectives, which should include:

- Identifying new and existing prospects

- Completing prospect profiles

- Assigning prospects

- Contacting prospects

- Engaging volunteers and board members

After you have set specific goals and objectives, you can build your strategy to meet them, using expertise from your key stakeholders.

Building your strategy of engagement

Part of every pre-event process includes identifying key prospects on the invitation list. Here are five proven strategies that will help make your event successful.

Strategy 1: Have your key stakeholders (CDO, major gift officers, and prospect researchers) review the event list to make sure that prospects, suspects, and other friends who have indicated interest in your organization are included. Once identified and confirmed, the prospect should be formally assigned to an appropriate staff member.

Strategy 2: After the invitations are sent, the assigned staff member will contact his assigned invitees and personally invite them to the event. As the event draws near, the key stakeholders must review the attendance list and identify prospects who are attending.

Strategy 3: Develop a strategy of engagement. Each fundraiser including board members and volunteers should identify at least three to five attendees with whom to engage in conversation about the organization. These prospects should be formally assigned to the fundraiser. Tracking prospect assignments and each contact will allow you to analyze the results of your targeted cultivation.

Strategy 4: Complete basic prospect research (total giving, first gift, last gift, largest gift, interests, last contact, relationships, employment) in an effort to pre-qualify your chosen three to five prospects. Doing your homework will allow you and your stakeholders to engage in meaningful conversation at the event.

Strategy 5: Your post-event process includes follow through and engaging your new friends in a way that raises their interest and inclination to give to your organization. You must document key points from your conversations in a contact report for each prospect. Include a next step with a timeline for completion. Through these ongoing contacts, you will be able to determine whether your new friend is qualified as a major gift prospect or is simply a loyal supporter of your organization.

Without a strategy of engagement, your event could become simply a line item in your budget. Sure, you may meet your net revenue goal for the event, but you may be missing out on a larger gift and a life-long relationship.

Can you afford another special event?

This is a question to consider, because when you tally your expenses (catering, linens, rentals, etc.) and combine it with staff time, you have to ask: Is it worth it?

Because event activities can start 12 months in advance, to evaluate the success of your event, you must analyze the number of hours spent by staff and the total pay attributed to those hours. You may find that the true cost of the event causes you to lose money.

The next question is: Will you be able to make up that loss with a well-planned strategy of engagement that leads to a major gift? By committing human resources beyond event staff and investing in prospect research, identification, qualification, and cultivation throughout the lifetime of the special event and after, you will not only increase your overall event income, but you also will increase the volume of your prospect pipeline. Imagine the number of qualified prospects that could come from a golf tournament, a gala, or a silent auction because you employed a strategy of engagement.

Until you have evaluated your existing events, you cannot effectively answer whether or not you can afford another one. And, after building an effective strategy of engagement, you may find that you don't need another one because your pipeline is overflowing with qualified prospects.

In any economy, but particularly in a tough economy, you must evaluate every event and determine whether that friend-raiser will meet your fundraising goals.

Chapter Six

Corporate Giving: How a Deal Trumps an Appeal

by Curt Weeden, President, Business & Nonprofit Strategies, Inc.

If nonprofit organizations pepper companies with generic appeals that have nothing to do with a corporation's business, don't look for a wave of new company contributions.

Fact: Corporate giving has been on the decline for more than two decades. Despite making well-publicized donations after headline-making catastrophic events such as the 2010 Haiti earthquake and 2011 Japanese tsunami, corporate contributions have dropped to about half of what they were 25 years ago.

During the 1980s, corporations deducted between 1.5 percent to 2.3 percent of pre-tax earnings for support of nonprofit programs and causes. Then in the 1990s, business generosity started slipping until it nosedived to around seven-tenths of 1 percent. Today, corporate philanthropy still hovers just below 1 percent of pre-tax profits — and there is no indication that companies are about to reinstate higher levels of charitable support.

Among the reasons for the decline:

1. CEO Myopia: Some company leaders at the top of the private sector food chain are clueless about how corporate donations can be advantageous to a business.

2. Muted Middle Management: Company executives charged with planning and carrying out philanthropic activities often can't or won't push for an increase in corporate giving.

3. Nonprofit Misfires: Organizations seeking help from companies don't take into account the "business relevance" factor when reaching out to the private sector.

While many companies fall short in recognizing the benefits of a well planned and administered contributions program, nonprofits can do a lot to prime the corporate philanthropy pump if they come forward with the right kind of business-relevant proposals. This chapter points out ways your organization can greatly improve its chances of success when seeking support from the business community.

Understanding why companies give

Before prospecting for corporate cash, products, or even employee volunteer time, think about what usually motivates a business to even think about lending a helping hand to a nonprofit. There are three primary reasons:

1. Moral and Social Responsibility: Corporations recognize they have some obligation to be socially responsible — but the definition of what "some" means differs from business to business.

2. Social Benefit: If for no other reason than to meet tax law requirements, companies want to be sure that all charitable donations they make actually address a legitimate social need (as defined by tax code).

3. Company Benefit: Research by McKinsey & Company shows what executives want a contribution to deliver back to the donor company:

- Enhanced reputation (70 percent)

- Bolstered employee skills (44 percent)

- Improved employee respect and pride for their company (42 percent)

- Differentiation from the company's competitors (38 percent)

Increasingly, organizations that move to the front of the line are those that best demonstrate how a contribution lines up with one or more of these bullet points.

Getting corporate support — what's the secret?

There are nearly one million 501(c)(3) charities in the United States, most of them hoping to bolster their donor lists with as many businesses as possible. More often than not, those hopes are dashed. Why? Because many of these nonprofits go about soliciting businesses the wrong way. Too often, appeals are made that are totally disconnected from a company's business interests or objectives. More and more corporations turn a deaf ear to this kind of "tin cup" fundraising.

Consider approaching a company with something different — not a traditional fundraising appeal but rather a deal that addresses a company's interests while at the same time advancing your organization's mission. Make a compelling case that clearly states:

- Why a business should carve out a portion of its earnings to assist your cause and program

- How your organization will use a corporation's support to turn that assistance into a "win-win" for both the company and your nonprofit

- What metrics, timetable, or other evaluation system will be used to validate that you have used a company's resources in an effective manner

How do you put together a "deal" likely to win business interest? Nonprofits that have the most success follow these few steps:

First, do your homework. Learn as much as you can about the company — not just its giving practices but also about its products and services, where it operates, its plans for the future, etc. Most businesses post an extraordinary amount of information on their websites. Publicly-held companies (there are around 13,000 of them) are the largest business donors in the nation and are required to be transparent in their operations. Business analyst services such as Hoovers add insight to a company's activities, hurdles, and opportunities. Be creative. Use this information to craft the framework for a business proposal.

Second, think outside the traditional corporate philanthropy box. Here's a reality check that many nonprofits simply don't grasp: the tax write-off benefits for a company's charitable gift and an ordinary business expense are the same (with some relatively minor exceptions). This means a corporation that supports your organization via its marketing division, its R&D office, or its advertising department gets the same tax advantage as if it made a donation through its contributions office. Although not always the case, many business departments and units outside the contributions office have more flexible budgets and will be more receptive to a "deal" if its business relevance is obvious.

Third, if the way into a business is through the corporation's contributions or company foundation office, consider the obvious. Many corporations have stated giving guidelines that include "we do not fund" provisions. For example, Boeing (like a vast number of other companies) does not fund individuals, political candidates, and religious organizations that further religious doctrine. Some companies flatly state they will not fund capital needs or endowments; others exclude support for pre-college programs. If your organization doesn't represent a comfortable fit for a company, then walk away. There are literally hundreds of thousands of "C," "S," and "LLC" businesses in the United States. Don't get bogged down with one ill-suited company when there are so many other prospects.

Fourth, don't overlook obvious clues. If a company announces that it will be expanding operations in a specific country, determine if/how your organization can help spark wider company name recognition in that location. When a company's giving guidelines include banner headlines about its societal interests, look for business-relevant ways to connect to the corporation. For example, Coca-Cola focuses on water stewardship, health, active lifestyles, community recycling, and education — does your organization have programming options that are in sync with these interests? Medtronic is a leading medical technology company that points much of its giving toward chronic disease initiatives and science education

— can you capitalize on these interests by incorporating them into a proposal that is relevant to the firm's business goals?

Fifth, decide what to ask for. It's not all about cash — many companies rely more on product as their "currency of choice" when it comes to making donations. In fact, the nation's leading corporate contributors (mainly pharmaceutical and software businesses) donated $2 worth of products for every $1 in cash! Added tax incentives account for one reason why product donations have become more popular. Some firms have also discovered that strategically placed product donations are more effective than product sampling or even a costly ad campaign.

Kellogg's Company is just one example of why product donations can be so beneficial to a company. Over a five-year period, it donated brand-name cereals and food products worth $125 million to the hunger-relief nonprofit, Feeding America. The contributed products get regularly spotlighted when the media covers Feeding America events throughout the nation.

Sixth, make sure your organization board members and senior staff are on the same page when it comes to seeking corporate support. That means making sure all the organization's stakeholders understand the value of reaching out to a corporation with a deal and not an appeal.

Conclusion

Corporations, particularly publicly held companies, have an obligation to be exceedingly careful and responsible for every contribution decision they make. Help corporations uphold that obligation by aligning your proposals with the company's mission and goals. Given shared visions, the nonprofits and businesses can form productive alliances that benefit both parties.

Chapter Seven

Best Practices and Cultivation Strategies for Planned Giving Programs

by Katherine Swank, J.D., Target Analytics Senior Consultant, Blackbaud

All successful planned giving programs are alike in three ways, because they all depend on:

1. Interaction

2. Interaction

3. Interaction

If you doubt this, make two phone calls to confirm my assertion. Your first call should be to a colleague at an organization that is struggling to establish an active or growing planned giving program. Ask if he gets out of the office to meet with prospects on a weekly basis. I expect the answer will be something like this: "No. I'd like to do that more. It's in my goals, but I'm so busy getting out the newsletter and rewriting the planned giving program brochure that I don't have time."

Your second call should be to someone who is known in your local community as having the best planned giving program around. Ask the same question. The successful planned gift officer will say: "Yes! It's my number one priority."

I assure you, if this simple test were the Mega Millions lottery, I'd be the winner. There is only one best practice in planned giving and it is interaction — getting out of the office.

Keeping on task

Many of us use a calendar or checklist of activities to keep ourselves on task. Using that same technique, you can make outreach to planned gift prospects simple. Set an appointment with yourself every day. Establish an easy-to-reach goal of talking with three people each workday who are somehow related to your planned giving efforts. Use these two techniques to get started:

1. Close your door, reserve a meeting room, or post a friendly note or door tag so that others will not disturb you. Asking Matters sells doorknob hangers that say, "I'm making fundraising calls. Please do not disturb." You can purchase them at www.askingmatters.com.

2. Schedule calling time as a meeting on your work calendar. Choose differing times during the week — early morning, early afternoon, late afternoon, and evening hours two to three nights a month.

If you haven't yet found your own "voice" in making outreach calls, read my suggestions for getting started in the Blackbaud white paper, *How to Talk with Donors about Planned Gifts*. It's free on www.blackbaud.com in Resources. Then set to work using this approach:

*   Monday 8:30 – 9:00 a.m. Call three people who have notified you of bequest expectancies in the past and just say "thank you" again.

*   Tuesday 11:00 – 11:30 a.m. Call three board or committee members or volunteers who have notified you of planned gift expectancies of any kind and say, "Was just thinking of you and your generosity and service to this organization and wanted to say thank you again."

*   Wednesday 1:45 – 2:15 p.m. Call three people who have recently responded to a marketing mailing or asked for information online to follow up on their inquiry; seek an appointment in person.

*   Thursday 2:30 – 3:00 p.m. Call three people who have been identified through a planned giving likelihood assessment as high-level

prospects; seek an appointment in person to say "thank you" and update them on current events at your organization.

- Friday 3:30 – 4:00 p.m. Walk to three people's desks in your office who are loyal supporters of the organization, have made a recent gift to the organization, have participated in a recent event with the organization, or have made a planned gift to the organization. Say, "On behalf of everyone here, thank you again for your thoughtful participation, not just as someone who works here, but as someone who really cares about our mission and those we serve."

With daily outreach comes the reward of building relationships with a multitude of others committed to the organization's mission success. Conversations about planned gift vehicles and how planned gifts make a difference at the organization will naturally occur. If you do what I've suggested, you'll be well on your way to mastering the key to planned giving success.

Start with the most common, most simple gift vehicles

If you've ever attended one of my presentations, you already know that I espouse keeping it simple. Since 90 percent of all planned gifts are bequests, it makes sense to start with them. If you are not familiar with the many ways that a bequest can be made, become so. That's simple as well. This list, while not exhaustive, constitutes the majority of planned gifts that you'll encounter during your career as a planned giving officer.

- Wills and trusts in which a person bequeaths something to your charity — 99 percent of the time it will be cash

- Life-insurance and retirement plans from which a person designates a percentage of the funds or a stated amount of the funds should be given to your charity upon their death — 100 percent of the time this will be cash

- Bank account and money market account funds that have been directed to be distributed to your charity through a pay-on-death provision — 100 percent of the time this will be cash

In reality, these are all bequests and, as you see, none of them are complicated. Sample language can easily be provided to help them in completing their desired gift. The payoff? Average planned gift amounts around $50,000 each in the U.S. and around $30,000 each in Canada.

Conversations with prospects about bequests are rarely technical but are, instead, emotional. Mission-driven donor stories and testimonials about others who have made these gifts are easy to share. Make your own bequest, and you can share your story. It's the easiest one to tell! You, more than any other person, understand the importance that deferred gifts will play at your nonprofit, and your leadership in making one will speak for itself. By putting your gift in place — not only at the organization where you work, but also at those organizations which you most care about — you will be a donor-peer, not just a solicitor. Complete a planned gift using a vehicle that works for you. Perhaps it's a gift in your will or trust, or a specific amount or percentage from a life insurance policy. Think of leaving a small bank account to your charity. With high average gift levels, your concentrated outreach efforts with the right prospects could put into place bequest gifts of more than $1 million in a short period of time.

Think of it this way: Working to secure one bequest gift of $50,000 each week creates an expectancy pool of $1 million in only 20 weeks! You can see why planned giving must be personal. Marketing through newsletters will never produce this result.

Adding other components to your success

Over time, incorporate the following components to add substantial results to your already spectacular outreach.

- As you get better at outreach, seek ways to better track and report your successes to those who matter. Written goals and objectives for both your personal activity and your program's expected current and future results are essential. If you don't have goals, you can't reach them, and you can't report on them either. Spend a little time making certain that your constituent relationship management system has coding and fields in place that help you track and report your personal outreach activity, gift intentions uncovered, and marketing efforts.

- Cultivate and solicit both your volunteer leadership and your organizational insiders for their personal planned gifts. A legacy leadership campaign is a fairly simple one, but it must be done well and it must be done right. Think of its structure like that of a capital campaign. Start with lead gifts and move down the giving pyramid. Your gift is in place and you now cultivate and solicit your fellow solicitors, if there are any. Together, you approach your internal leader and ask him or her to make a planned gift as well. From there, your leader and development head solicit your volunteer leadership. A peer staff person solicits other key staff. Success comes from planning, communicating the plan to the intended planned gift prospects, and personal (face-to-face) solicitation — the most important element of all.

- Establish meaningful gift acceptance policies and lead an annual review of them. The policies inform your outreach for the right types of gifts and also keep your goals and reporting elements on track as well. If you don't have policies in place, you should plan to correct that. Read my white paper, *Why You Need Gift Acceptance Policies*, to understand their importance and how to get started. You'll find it in the White Papers and Tip Sheets area at www.blackbaud.com.

- Use data and statistical analytics to focus your efforts on those most likely to make a planned gift to your organization. Data analysis is a science and requires more than anecdotal record selects to succeed in identifying your best prospects. It's a fact that most people actively engaged in estate planning are younger than we think. They are also more philanthropically minded than their parents and grandparents, who waited longer to make their legacy gifts. As a result, rudimentary formulas based on age and loyalty have been replaced by sophisticated analytic modeling products. Predictive giving behavior models separate great prospects in your database from unlikely prospects and, more importantly, identify "must see" prospects. A recent example: The Salvation Army In North and South Carolina used predictive modeling and statistical analysis to identify potential donors likely to make a bequest to the Salvation Army. The effort uncovered $4.2 million in new bequests not already identified. Without the use of modeling for prospect identification, these gifts would most likely not have been discovered.

- Finally, establish a recognition and stewardship program that provides the same or similar treatment of donors as your organization's major gift recognition and stewardship programs. Like all other donors, planned gift donors must be tended and thanked on a regular basis. More likely than not, the legacy gift they have established for you will be their largest gift to your organization. Treatment that belies or ignores this fact is unforgiveable. These are major donors. Be certain that you respect them as such and they will reward you with larger current gifts, longer gift-giving cycles, and increased affiliation. Disregard them and they will take their gifts — all of them — to another organization.

Conclusion

The most successful component of your planned giving program is not marketing, but a strong and very proactive outreach effort. Phone calls, personal visits, voice-to-voice, and face-to-face contact must be the norm — not the exception — for your planned giving communications. Understand that people give to people, not to marketing campaigns.

People will soon learn that when your door is closed, it's not to keep them out, but to allow you to have meaningful and private conversations with legacy donors and prospects. Stand firm with your commitment to devote 30 minutes to one hour each day for phone time. This effort is the foundation of your personal and programmatic success. No other activity replaces it, and nothing should get in your way of completing it. Let's be frank, while editing a newsletter article may seem important, the activity in itself will not secure one appointment for you. On the other hand, daily phone calls will secure many.

Set a goal of one to five appointments per week, depending on your other duties. Even more than phone calls, face-to-face meetings pay off. Some of your appointments serve as cultivation for future gifts, others are solicitations to make gifts, and others concern stewardship of gifts that have already been completed. If you doubt this formula and need confirmation from an actual donor, check out the brief donor interview *How One Donor Spends $50,000 Annually with Planned Gifts of Over One Million*, on www.nonprofitexpert.com. Read it, pick up the phone, and make a call!

About the Authors

Katya Andresen
Chief Operating Officer and Chief Strategy Officer, Network for Good

Katya is chief strategy officer of Network for Good, as well as a speaker, author, and blogger about nonprofit marketing, online outreach, social media, and fundraising. In addition, she is an adjunct professor of communications at American University's Key Certificate Program and serves on the board of NTEN. Katya has trained thousands of causes in effective engagement, and her marketing materials for nonprofits have won national and international awards. She is the author of the book, *Robin Hood Marketing: Stealing Corporate Savvy to Sell Just Causes* and was featured in the e-book, *Nine Minds of Marketing*. She is also an author featured in *People to People Fundraising - Social Networking and Web 2.0 for Charities*. Fundraising Success Magazine named her Fundraising Professional of the Year in 2007, and she has since become one of its regular columnists. Before joining Network for Good, she was senior vice president of Sutton Group, a marketing and communications firm and a marketing consultant overseas in Ukraine. She also worked for CARE International. Katya traces her passion for good causes to the enormous social need she witnessed as a journalist. She was a foreign correspondent for Reuters News and Television in Asia, and for Associated Press in Africa.

Melissa Bank Stepno
Target Analytics Senior Consultant, Blackbaud

Melissa joined Blackbaud in 2008, following the acquisition of Kintera. For more than a decade, she has helped hundreds of nonprofits with designing strategy and implementation plans for predictive modeling and database screening projects. Previously, Melissa served as a senior development researcher at Boston University where she was responsible for managing wealth screenings of more than 100,000 records. Melissa sits on the boards of Brandeis University's Alumni Association, the New England Development Researchers Association, and the Association of Fundraising Professionals Northern New England Chapter. She received her BA from Brandeis University and MA in Arts Administration and Higher Education Administration from Boston University. You can contact her at Melissa.Stepno@ blackbaud.com.

Amy Braiterman
Principal Strategy Consultant, Blackbaud

Amy supports customers with their peer-to-peer fundraising events with a process she refers to as "data-driven strategy." Amy's data driven strategy analyzes how effective event participants are using online fundraising tools and takes those results to develop an event fundraising plan. Prior to joining Blackbaud, Amy earned her fundraising stripes managing events for The Leukemia & Lymphoma Society, Alzheimer's Association, and Share Our Strength. She shares her fundraising know how through her popular blog FriendsAskingAmy.com, by hosting educational webinars and speaking at customer conferences

Danielle Brigida
Manager of Social Media, National Wildlife Federation

Danielle is a self-proclaimed wildlife geek and works as the manager of social media for the National Wildlife Federation. She actively engages a wide range of constituents using a mixture of online tools and social networking sites. An early adopter of social media with creative, engaging campaigns, Danielle has been recognized as: 10 Green Women We Love by Greenopia; one of the 75 Environmentalists to follow by Mashable; Top 50 green people to follow on Twitter by Greenopolis; A featured Changemaker by Change.org; A Measurement Maven of the Month by Katie Paine. She is a sought after speaker with more than 20 appearances over the past year. She's spoken at conferences such as South by Southwest (SXSW), PR News Digital Media Summit, Blog World, Nonprofit

Technology Conference, Netroots Nation, as well as several webinars. Additionally, Danielle has been interviewed about her social media experience by the New York Times, USA Today, The Nonprofit Times, Fast Company, Washington Post, Mashable, GreenTalk Radio, Fundraising Success Magazine, Beth's Blog, and several other popular blogs. Danielle graduated from Christopher Newport University with a BA in Technical Writing with minors in Biology and Communications.

Mark Davis
Director of Enterprise Internet Solutions, Blackbaud

Mark has worked directly with many of the largest nonprofits in the industry, such as American Heart Association, Big Brothers Big Sisters of America, and Arthritis Foundation, helping to deploy online fundraising solutions. As one of the original architects of Friends Asking Friends® technology, he has actively participated in the development of the Blackbaud Sphere™ product. He received his BA in engineering from Duke University and a MA in Engineering from Stanford University.

Casey Golden
CEO, Small Act

A lifetime entrepreneur, Casey started his first business at the age of 11 and has since started many successful companies, including the most recent, Parature, a Customer Relationship Management software company which grew to over 120 employees. His current venture, Small Act, helps nonprofits and associations nurture key relationships online with its social media software tools, Thrive, and Profile Builder. A frequent speaker at national events who also donates his time to serve on several nonprofit advisory boards, Casey contributed a chapter to *Do Your Giving While You Are Living*. He recently won the "35 Under 35" award for top entrepreneurs in greater D.C. and was honored as a leader for social change as part of the Class of 2009 of Greater D.C. Cares. Casey lives in Northern Virginia with his wife, Beverley, and four-year-old twins, Tristan and Lilyrose.

Tom Krackeler
Former Vice President of Common Ground, Convio

Tom has spent the last 14 years developing web technology that enables nonprofits to acquire, engage, and retain supporters online. During his time at Convio, Tom led Convio's Common Ground product line, a nonprofit constituent relationship management solution. He currently serves on the board for NTEN and has worked in the nonprofit sector at the Environmental Defense Fund and as a consultant with Accenture. Tom has a BA in Political Science and Philosophy from Duke University and an MPP in Public Policy from UC Berkeley.

Susan Ulrich McLaughlin, CFRE
Principal Consultant, Blackbaud

Susan brings more than 16 years of fundraising and nonprofit administration experience to her role as a principal consultant with Blackbaud. Susan is responsible for leading enterprise-level implementations of Blackbaud solutions within the Healthcare and Human Services vertical. Prior to joining Blackbaud, Susan led the J.C. Blair Memorial Hospital Foundation in Pennsylvania as its first executive director. She was responsible for all aspects of foundation management including fundraising, financial management, database management, policy development, fund distribution, marketing, and public relations. Susan began her career in fundraising at Penn State University and directed major and annual giving programs at Juniata College. Previously, she served as vice president for advancement at Allegheny Lutheran Social Ministries. She is a charter member of the Association of Fundraising Professionals, Allegheny Mountains Chapter, and was recognized as the chapter's first Outstanding Fundraising Professional in 2006. In 2009, Susan received recognition as Colleague of the Quarter by her Blackbaud peers. Susan holds a BA from Gettysburg College. She received her CFRE credential in 2000 and serves as a subject matter expert for CFRE, International.

Katherine Swank, J.D.
Senior Consultant, Target Analytics, a Blackbaud Company

Katherine joined the Target Analytics team in 2007 with more than 25 years of legal and nonprofit management experience. Prior, she was the national director of gift planning at the National Multiple Sclerosis Society, where she provided fundraising consulting services to the Society's chapter leadership and development staff for six years. Katherine has raised over $215 million during her career, with a focus on planned and major giving. As an affiliate faculty member of Regis University's Masters in Global Nonprofit Leadership program, Katherine teaches courses on wealth and philanthropy in America. She is a member of the Arizona State Bar and a past president of the Colorado Planned Giving Roundtable. In 2010, Katherine was inducted into Target Analytics' Hall of Fame, which recognizes team members who epitomize excellence in service and was named as one of the top ten participant-rated speakers at Blackbaud's 2010 Conference for Nonprofits. She earned a BA in counseling and education from the University of Northern Colorado and a Doctor of Jurisprudence from Drake University Law School. You can contact Katherine at Katherine.Swank@blackbaud.com.

Curt Weeden
President, Business & Nonprofit Strategies, Inc.

Curt is recognized as one of the nation's leading experts in the philanthropy and social responsibility fields. He speaks frequently to nonprofit and business audiences on philanthropy trends and how business-nonprofit alliances can generate social change while addressing private sector interests.

Curt founded and served as chief executive of the Association of Corporate Contributions Professionals (ACCP), the national trade group representing corporate contributions, community relations, and employee volunteer managers from over 150 companies. Member companies are responsible for over $20 billion in annual corporate cash and product contributions. In

1999, he launched the Contributions Academy, which became the principal management education resource for corporate grant makers in the U.S. and in many countries abroad. The Academy became part of ACCP in July 2005. Before launching the Academy, Curt served as vice president for Johnson & Johnson and managed that corporation's $150 million contributions program. Before joining J&J, he headed a consulting firm that provided external relations and merger/acquisition services to several of the nation's largest businesses including Bank of America, General Motors, Merck, and Xerox.

About Blackbaud and the Desktop Reference Series

Serving the nonprofit and education sectors for 30 years, Blackbaud (NASDAQ: BLKB) combines technology and expertise to help organizations achieve their missions. Blackbaud works with more than 27,000 customers in more than 60 countries that support higher education, healthcare, human services, arts and culture, faith, the environment, independent education, animal welfare, and other charitable causes. The company offers a full spectrum of cloud-based and on-premise software solutions, and related services for organizations of all sizes including: fundraising, eMarketing, social media, advocacy, constituent relationship management (CRM), analytics, financial management, and vertical-specific solutions. Using Blackbaud technology, these organizations raise more than $100 billion each year. Recognized as a top company by Forbes, InformationWeek, and Software Magazine, and honored by Best Places to Work, Blackbaud is headquartered in Charleston, South Carolina and has employees throughout the US, and in Australia, Canada, Hong Kong, Mexico, the Netherlands, and the United Kingdom.

Look for more relevant topics in our Desktop Reference series, or visit www.blackbaud.com/DesktopReference for other valuable tools and information.